MW01264444

# GROUNDHOG SECRETS

## by Lieve Snellings

Everything You Always
Wanted to Know about Woodchucks

**Margot the Groundhog and her
Nort-American Squirel Family - 2**

This book is dedicated to all animal lovers.
Margot gives a high four to all who want
to know everything about groundhogs.

A special thanks to Tina, Pam, Monique, Kristie and
Stella. You all are wonderful.

Photos and graphics: Lieve Snellings
Text: Lieve Snellings
Translation: Tina Gianoulis, 2017
Editor: Pamela Peniston
Narration: Margot, the groundhog
Available in e-book and paperback
ISBN-13: 978-1546813033
ISBN-10: 1546813039

This is the second book in the
Series 'Margot the Groundhog
and her North-American Squirrel
Family'

All rights reserved. No part of this publication may be reproduced and / or published by print, electronic, photocopying, microfilm or any other manner whatsoever without the written permission of the author.

I hope you have
lots of fun reading,
looking at the pictures and learning!

\*These are snow geese!

"Wait! Don't go! Sérafine must come and pick up a letter for Quebec."

5

"Margot, Margot ...
I have mail for you!"
cried Serafine the
postwoman.

"This letter was accidentally sent
way up to the Artic Circle, and, since
Quebec is on our way South, I promised to
bring it to you myself."

A letter? What fun!
It is surely from Marie
and Lowieske*.
Now I understand why
I haven't heard from them.

* See the book: 'MARGOT GETS AN UNEXPECTED VISIT'

Lummen, Belgium April 25, 2017

Dearest Margot,

We returned home after our trip to Chateau-Richer.
We think a lot about all those beautiful days we spent
together.

We were super-happy with your letter. Your project is
great! Yes, please write your book on your life with its
ups and downs.' We want to order a copy. Will you
send it to us when it's ready? Here, everyone we talked
to when we came home from vacation wants to know
more about you.

Big kisses and looking forward to hearing from you.
Marie

Marie

LOWIESKE

And I thought they had already forgotten me! No, on the contrary, they want to know everything about woodchucks like me. Well, this letter makes me want to start writing right away!

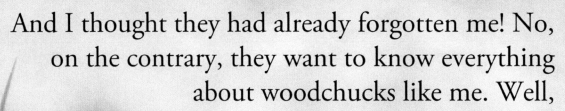

There are fourteen types of marmots in the world. We all look alike, but unlike many other species of marmots, we groundhogs are solitary. That means we really like to live alone.

I am Margot, a groundhog, one of the types of marmots.

All marmots live in the northern hemisphere. We woodchucks live in North America.

I live in a field in Chateau-Richer, near the St. Lawrence River and the beautiful city of Quebec.

9

We are rodents. We grind our food by moving our jaw from front to back. (A rabbit, who also has large teeth in front, but who is not a rodent, moves its jaw from side to side.) We hold the food with our front legs that are very flexible. (Rabbits don't have that skill either).

We are only active during the day, especially in the early morning and afternoon. We can eat up to 1.1 pounds (or half a kilo) of food a day. That's a lot of work, chewing and digesting. Our diet contains green plants, like grass, clover, alfalfa, dandelions, and plantains, along with seeds and fruits, such as berries. We also like carrots and corn. Farmers say that we not only eat their crops, but we do a lot of damage in the fields with our pathways.

We have two pairs of sharp teeth called incisors that are white and pointed.

We are herbivores, but from time to time we like to nibble on grasshoppers and meals like snails, caterpillars and insects.

Occasionally, we steal the eggs of birds nesting on the ground and eat them. They taste so good!

In the winter, people put salt on the roads to melt the ice, and salt contains sodium, which we think is delicious. When the snowplow passes, it pushes the snow filled with sodium to the side of the road. To our joy, the sodium remains when the snow melts in early spring. We're just as fond of that as you are of ice cream. That's why, after our hibernation, you see us nibble on the roadside. But that is dangerous! Many of us can be hit by cars that way.

Besides the risks of the road, humans, foxes and other raptors are the greatest dangers for us. Most of the victims are groundhog babies. Young adults can usually escape predators.

Like all living
beings, of course
we need water.
We do not
often drink
from a spring
or a stream.
Instead, we can
get all the water we
need from plants and
the dew we find on the
grass and leaves.

In the early spring we eat snow.

14

Our skin is a grayish brown color. Each hair is gray at the bottom, black in the center and white at the ends. At our abdomen and legs, our fur looks orange brown because that's the middle part of our hairs' color there.

15

When danger threatens, we try to avoid a fight by quickly returning to our burrow. But that does not always work. If necessary, we defend ourselves tooth and nail.

When we are afraid, we bow our backs. The hair on our tail stands up so that it looks like a spiky hairbrush. We strike the ground with our stiffly upright tail and make a chattering noise with our teeth.

We also send a shrill whistle sound to warn others of the danger. That is why, in Quebec, we are called 'siffleux' (whistler), and English speakers call us 'whistle-pigs'.

I have just been interrupted by my neighbor running in to say, "Before going any further, shouldn't you introduce our entire family of Sciuridae first?"

He's right, of course!
I will you tell you about it.

The scientific name for woodchuck is *Marmota Monax*. The English-speaking people call us groundhog, and Francophones say marmotte commune. We are a subgroup of the marmots, belonging to the family of squirrels, whose name is SCIURIDAE (pronounced: ski uridaaj). Yes, you can believe it! The groundhog is really related to all the different types of squirrels, including the small chipmunk and prairie dogs, which live a little further away.

I will ask my little cousins who live in Quebec to give you a word of explanation.

"I am Fiston, the smallest Sciuridae. In Quebec everyone knows me as le petit suisse (little Swiss). This is because the first French settlers who saw me here thought my coat looked like the uniform of the Swiss Guards at the Vatican.

An adult tamia (the official scientific name) or chipmunk (as English speakers say) weighs 1 to 2 ounces (35 to 53 g) and measures 4 to 5 inches (10 to 13 cm). Its tail is 3 to 4 inches (8 to 10 cm) in length."

19

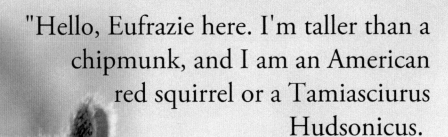

"Hello, Eufrazie here. I'm taller than a chipmunk, and I am an American red squirrel or a Tamiasciurus Hudsonicus.

An adult red squirrel weighs around half a pound (200 to 250 g) and measures 11 to 14 inches (28 to 35 cm), including our tail that is 4 to 6 inches (10 to 15 cm) long.

We have reddish fur and a white belly. During the summer, a black line separates the two colors."

"I am Philomene and I belong to the family of Gray Squirrels or Sciurus Carolinensis.

Twice a year we change clothes. We have a summer coat and a winter coat. Our tail changes only once, in July. When it rains, we spread our tail over our head like an umbrella. So we can stay dry while we eat.

And to keep warm during the night, we wrap ourselves up in our tail. It falls like a blanket around us. It's nice and warm!"

21

"I'm Germaine, the black version of a gray squirrel like Philomene.
Due to the large amount of melanin* in our black skin, we lose less body heat than squirrels of lighter color. There are also gray albino squirrels that are completely white.
The Gray Squirrel is the largest squirrel that lives in the native trees of the eastern United States and Canada."

*Melanin is an organic pigment in the skin. A pigment is a substance that reflects a color.

Germaine
the Acrobat

The gray squirrel
measures 18 to 26 inches
(45 to 65 cm), including
the tail, which is 8 inches
(20 cm) in length. This
helps to maintain balance so
they can perform fantastic
jumps. Also, their tails can
be used to give signals to
other squirrels.

Adult gray
squirrels
weigh from
1 to 2 pounds
(455 to 800 g)
and can reach speeds of
15 mph (25 km/h).

23

You can see now that our family is very diverse. After introducing my distant cousins, it is time to continue talking about us, the groundhogs.

We move both on top of and under the ground. We can also climb trees. In addition, we are excellent swimmers.

While we are slower and heavier than the rest of the family, we can reach speeds of 9 to 10 mph (15 to 17 km/h), thanks to our front legs, which are very strong.

We are the most widespread rodents in North America and the largest burrowing mammals in the eastern part of the continent.

Of all the rodents that live here, only beavers and porcupines are bigger than us.

Our size varies from 16 to 24 inches (40 to 65 cm), including our short, bushy tail, which measures from 3 to 6 inches (7.5 to 15 cm).

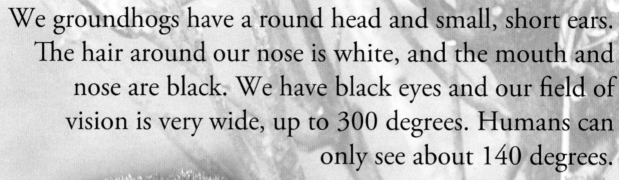

We groundhogs have a round head and small, short ears. The hair around our nose is white, and the mouth and nose are black. We have black eyes and our field of vision is very wide, up to 300 degrees. Humans can only see about 140 degrees.

We have strong back legs with black feet that have five toes, all with claws. The underside of the foot is bare and has six pads.

Our hind legs are 3 to 4 inches (7.5 to 10 cm) long. That makes it easy for us to stand upright. We do it fairly often so that we can keep an eye on our environment.

27

Our front legs are short but strong and have only four fingers. Fortunately, our claws are strong and well developed. They make it easier to dig our burrow. Thanks to them, we can move 550 pounds  (250 kg) of soil within a few days and build a complex of 20 to 33 feet (six to ten meter) corridors. The main entrance has a width of about 1 foot (30 cm). The bedroom is approximately 1.5 feet (50 cm) wide and 1 foot (30 cm) high.

We make at least one main corridor which can be
recognized by the pile of dirt
at the exit, but which
cannot be seen at
the entrance
of the side
passages.

These serve as escape routes in case of danger and are
also used as links between the different fields where we
will eat. The bedroom of our burrow has three functions:
it is a place to rest, to hibernate, and to raise our young
in the spring.

29

Next to the bedroom, there is
an extra room that serves as a toilet.

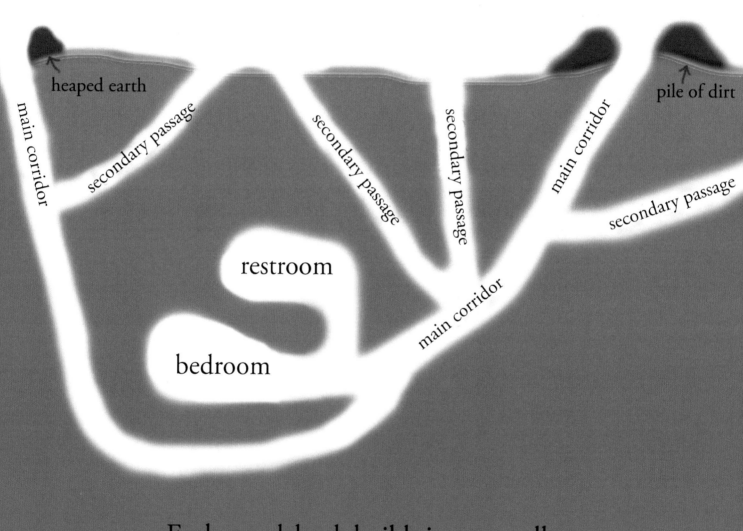

heaped earth

main corridor

secondary passage

secondary passage

secondary passage

main corridor

pile of dirt

secondary passage

restroom

bedroom

main corridor

Each woodchuck builds its own gallery
structure. Each of our houses is different.

Our winter burrow is located in a wooded area in the northern part of our territory. In the summer, we move south into more open areas. This shelter is shallower, but has several secondary passages to escape in case of danger.

Usually we go back to our old burrow every year. When we leave it, it can also be used as a refuge by other furry animals such as rats, mice, skunks and raccoons.
And very occasionally you'll see a gnome there!

By the end of the summer we eat as much as we can to build up our body fat.

In six months, our weight -normally 4.5 to 9 pounds (two to four kilos)- doubles. We need this thick layer of fat in order to have enough reserves for the long winter months.

As soon as autumn arrives, we begin digging our winter burrow. Because of the cold we make this space deeper than our summerhouse. We build it about 5 feet (a meter and a half deep), so that the hollow remains below the freezing layer. We block up the tunnel from the inside with earth and grass. This way, we can better protect ourselves against the cold.

Each year, we hope for a thick layer of snow to give extra insulation over our burrow.

33

We have
the deepest
hibernation.
Neither the bear
nor the badger falls
asleep so completely.

In order not to lose heat,
we roll up in a ball to sleep.
Our hibernation lasts more than five months.

At this point, all our vital functions slow down to consume
a minimum of calories. Our heart rate drops to five beats
per minute instead of eighty, as it is when we are awake.
Our temperature drops to 37.4 °F (3 °C), and our breathing
is reduced from forty times a minute to only twice a minute.

Today, doctors are very interested in these phenomena of hibernation which reduce the temperature of our body, our heart rate, and our breath.

If humans could do this, even for a short time, it could lead to dramatic improvements in health care. Some surgeries and other medical treatments could then be carried out without anesthesia. Medical researchers continue to try to understand our hibernation process.

35

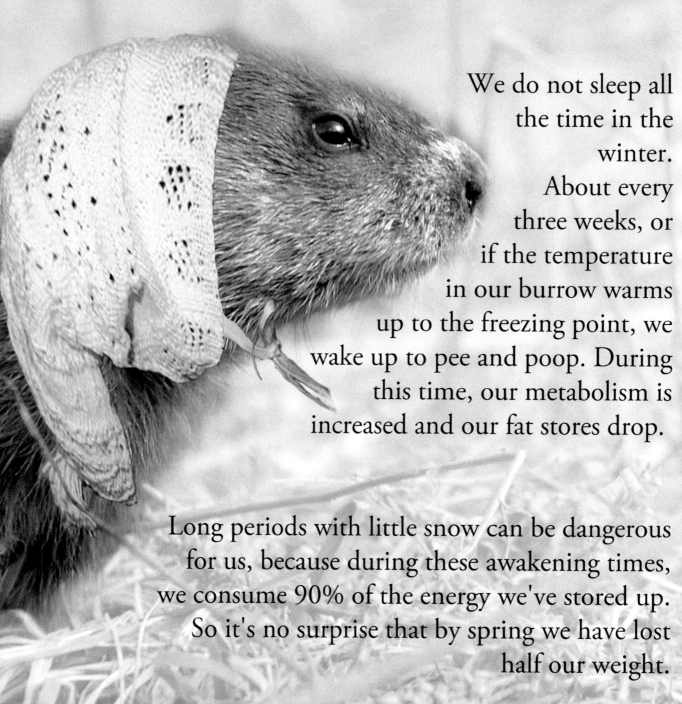

We do not sleep all the time in the winter. About every three weeks, or if the temperature in our burrow warms up to the freezing point, we wake up to pee and poop. During this time, our metabolism is increased and our fat stores drop.

Long periods with little snow can be dangerous for us, because during these awakening times, we consume 90% of the energy we've stored up. So it's no surprise that by spring we have lost half our weight.

After the hibernation time spent in the dark,
it is always nice to see the light. And it's a
real pleasure to feel the sun on our fur!

In spring, food is still scarce. That's another reason we need to build up our body fat before hibernation.

Our territory is about 10 acres (0.3 to 4 hectares or up to six soccer or football fields) and the territory of the male often overlaps that of one or more females.

The mating season begins immediately after hibernation. It is the only short period in which we do not sleep alone.

We have one pregnancy a year. The gestation period lasts from 28 to 32 days. At the end of April or early May, we have from two to nine little woodchucks. They are called kits or pups. Fortunately nature has provided groundhog mothers with four pairs of breasts to feed them.

Baby groundhogs have no hair and are blind at birth. They measure about 4 inches (10 cm) and weigh 1 ounce (30 g). After a month, they open their eyes. They begin to crawl, and their

hair begins to grow. From that day on, they grow up very quickly. In six weeks, they already weigh 1 pound, 5 ounces (600 g) and go out for the first time to cautiously explore their surroundings.

Only mom takes care of the baby woodchucks.

After three months, by the end of next spring at the latest, the groundhog's children become too big and must leave the house.

Woodchucks take a year to become adults. After that, female groundhogs can have babies, but they usually wait two years before becoming mothers.

* The teeth of all rodents continue to grow, but those of this little one were crooked which has certainly caused a problem.

42

# *Groundhog Day: legend or reality?*

For many Americans, February 2 is Groundhog Day. An old folk tradition says that if Fred the marmot (Quebec) or Phil the groundhog (USA) comes out of hibernation and sees his shadow, he gets frightened and returns quickly to sleep, as he sees this as a sign of bad weather. If the woodchuck does not see its shadow, spring is close at hand!

Today, everyone is convinced that this is just an old legend, probably invented by the first settlers who were eager for spring to begin. In the Old Continent, Europe, February 2 is celebrated as the moment when the days begin to lengthen. It is the day of hope for a new life and rebirth. But in Quebec and many places in the United States, in February there is still snow everywhere and woodchucks will not wake from hibernation until March (even later in the far north). In any case, the legend of groundhog's day makes a great story for long cold winter evenings.

Here ends the story of Margot the woodchuck.

Do you have more questions about the lives of groundhogs?

Or maybe you have a suggestion...
Don't hesitate to tell me!

Please leave a comment on
the Amazon site to say what
you think of this book.
Here is the link: http://smarturl.it/0psllg

Thank you so much!

Bye-Bye!

Margot en Lieve

45

# Other books in the series 'Margot the Groundhog and her North-American Squirrel Family' by Lieve Snellings

*Book 1:*

## Margot gets an unexpected visit

Asin : B01E0FL2HK
ISBN: 978-1532877650

"A Beautiful story about being different. The photography and story are both stunning and humorous." - Rich Linville

The photography is good and Lieve Snellings does a tremendous job of touching on critical social issues, while keeping the story suitable for children. Margot the groundhog should be a character on a children's tv show – Larry Singleton

*Book 3 is forseen for end of October 2019*

## Margot has to go to bed (this is a work title, so it can change)

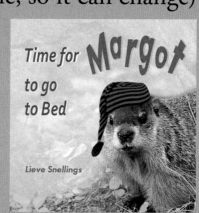

She cries and asks how she can survive tnext winter?
Lucky she has friends.
Margot is sad because she has to start hibernation. That is very unusual! Her friends help her find out why she's in tears. Together they find some solutions, and soon Margot can go to sleep with a smile.
Want to find out more?